EXCEL Formulas

and Functions

2024

140 Most Popular Shortcuts and tricks for Beginners to Experts

Steven M. Rader

EXCEL Formulas and Functions 2024

Table of Contents

Introduction

Microsoft Excel, commonly called Excel" is a powerful tool vital in today's business landscape and beyond. With its range of functions, Excel helps users effectively manage data, perform calculations, and create appealing reports. Whether you're a student or simply looking to boost your productivity, Excel offers benefits and applications. In this section, we will explore why Microsoft Excel holds immense significance in the contemporary world.

The Versatility of Excel

Excel is a tool that can handle various jobs because of its adaptability. Excel remains the preferred tool for professionals in multiple industries, whether you need to manage budgets and financial models, carry out simple calculations or complicated data analysis, or support project management and data visualization. It is popularly known and used.

Universal Applicability

Lots of industries use MS Excel. Whether you work in finance, marketing, healthcare, education, engineering, or any other sector, Excel does the job very well.

Efficiency and Accuracy

One of Excel's primary advantages is its ability to enhance efficiency and accuracy. Tedious manual calculations become automated, reducing the risk of human error. You can create complex formulas and functions that instantly update with changing inputs, ensuring consistent accuracy in your work.

Data Organization and Management

Excel is a superb tool for organizing and managing data. With its intuitive spreadsheet interface, you can create structured datasets, sort and filter information effortlessly, and perform powerful data manipulations. This capability is vital for businesses that rely on data-driven decision-making.

Visualization and Reporting

Data visualization is important in effective communication in today's world. Microsoft Excel excels in this regard. Making educational graphs, tables, and charts is a simple way to display data in a way that is both readable and aesthetically pleasing. This helps to convey complex information to colleagues, clients, or stakeholders in an easy-to-understand visual.

Collaboration and Sharing

In today's interconnected world, collaboration is key. Excel provides features for real-time collaboration, making it possible for multiple users to work on the same workbook simultaneously, whether in the same office or continents apart. Additionally, sharing Excel files is straightforward, allowing for seamless communication and information exchange.

Career Advancement

Proficiency in Microsoft Excel is a sought-after skill in the job market. Employers value candidates who can navigate Excel efficiently, which signifies problem-solving abilities, analytical thinking, and the capacity to handle data-related tasks. Excel proficiency can significantly enhance career prospects

In conclusion, Microsoft Excel is indispensable in today's professional landscape. Its versatility and applicability across industries make it an essential tool for individuals and organizations. This book is a playbook on how to navigate this powerful tool and develop the fundamental skills to help you become savvy and level up your Excel game.

What you'll get from this book.

In this book, we'll cover:

1. **Getting Started with Excel:** We'll walk you through the process of launching Excel and understanding its fundamentals.

2. **Excel functions and formulas:** Familiarize yourself with the formulas and commands that make Excel perform calculations.

3. **Managing data in Excel:** Learn how to perform tasks related to data management. Functions like sorting data, filtering data, and the like.

4. **Excel formatting:** Explore essential procedures to optimize the Excel experience.

5. **Excel visuals:** Discover how to create and customize visuals like charts and graphs in Excel.

6. **Excel shortcuts and formula tips:** comprehensive list of handy shortcuts and formulas to save time and boost your productivity.

Chapter 1
Excel Fundamentals

Setting Up Your Excel Environment

It's imperative to start with the fundamentals of creating your Excel environment before we go into the intriguing world of Excel functions and formulae. You will be guided through the first few stages in this chapter so that you are comfortable and knowledgeable about the Excel interface, options, and necessary adjustments.

You will be able to use Excel with efficiency and confidence by the end of this chapter. Your Excel journey will be easier and more productive since you'll have a strong basis for configuring your Excel environment. So, let's start this thrilling journey and utilize all of Microsoft Excel's capabilities!

Understanding Workbooks and Worksheets

What is a Workbook?

A workbook in Excel is like a digital notebook that contains your data, calculations, and charts. It consists of one or more worksheets (also known as sheets). Take these actions to create a new worksheet:

1. Open Excel.

2. Select "File" located in the upper-left corner.

3. Select "New."

4. Choose "Blank Workbook."

5. A new workbook will open with a default worksheet (Sheet 1).

Select Blank workbook

Worksheets

Worksheets in Microsoft Excel are referred to as single pages within a workbook where you input and store data. Follow these steps to add or delete worksheets:

Adding Worksheets: Right-click on a worksheet tab at the bottom and click "Insert" or click the plus icon.

Deleting Worksheets: Right-click on the worksheet tab and click "Delete."

Image of an Excel Worksheet

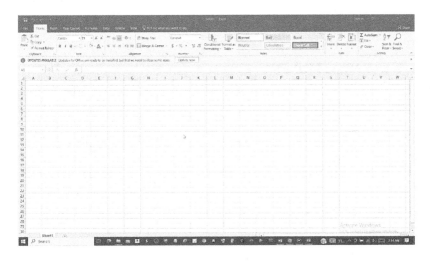

Navigating the Excel Interface

Ribbon and Tabs

The Ribbon is the toolbar at the top of the Excel window, organized into tabs (e.g., Home, Insert, Page Layout). Each tab contains related commands. To navigate:

- Click on a tab to access its commands.
- Explore each tab's groups (e.g., Font, Alignment) for specific actions.

Image of an Excel Ribbon

Quick Access Toolbar

The Quick Access Toolbar is located above the Ribbon and provides quick access to frequently used commands. To customize it:

- On the Quick Access Toolbar, click the dropdown arrow.
- Select "More Commands."
- Add or remove commands as needed.

1.2.3 Cells, Rows, and Columns

Excel organizes data in a grid of cells, where each cell is identified by a unique cell address (e.g., A1, B2). A row is the horizontal alignment of data while a vertical alignment of data is called a column. Data in a column describes a field of information all entities possess while data in a row contains information that describes a single entity. To navigate:

- Click on a cell to select it.
- To navigate between cells, use the arrow keys.
- Click the column or row headers to select entire columns or rows.

Image of Excel Rows and Columns

Entering and Formatting Data

Data Entry Basics

To enter data into a cell:

1. Click on the desired cell.

2. Begin typing.

3. Press "Enter" to move to the next cell or use the arrow keys.

4. To edit a cell, double-click on it or press F2.

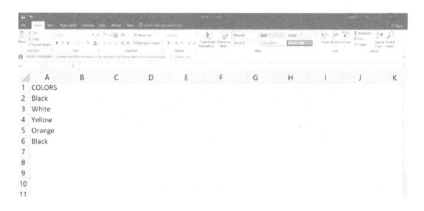

Image of Excel Worksheet with Data

Basic Formatting

To format cell contents:

1. Select the cell(s) you want to format.

2. Use the commands in the "Font" and "Alignment" groups on the Home tab to change font, font size, bold, italics, alignment, and more.

AutoFill and Flash Fill

AutoFill: Excel can automatically fill in a series of data (e.g., numbers, dates, days of the week).

1. Enter the starting value in a cell.
2. Hover over the bottom-right corner of the cell until you see a small square (the Fill Handle).
3. Click and drag to autofill adjacent cells.

Flash Fill: Excel can recognize patterns and fill data accordingly.

1. Start typing data that follows a pattern.
2. Press "Ctrl + E," and Excel will attempt to auto-fill the rest of the data.

Saving Your Work

Saving Workbooks

To save your Excel workbook:

1. Select "File" in the top-left menu.
2. Select "Save" or "Save As."
3. Choose a location on your computer.
4. Enter a filename.
5. Select a file format (e.g., Excel Workbook (.xlsx)).
6. Click "Save."

AutoSave and Versions

AutoSave: AutoSave automatically saves your changes as you work. To enable or disable it:

1. Click "File."
2. Select "Options."
3. Go to "Save."
4. Adjust AutoSave settings.

Versions: Multiple versions of your workbook can be saved in Excel.

1. Click "File."
2. Select "Info."
3. Choose "Manage Workbook" and "Version History."

By following these detailed steps and explanations, you acquire a solid understanding of Excel's fundamental concepts and functions. This foundational knowledge will serve as a strong basis for further exploration of Excel's capabilities in subsequent chapters.

Chapter 2

Basic Functions and Formulas

You may make calculations, examine data, and automate processes using the Excel functions and formulas we'll explore in this chapter. Anyone wishing to utilize Excel's full potential must possess these core skills.

Introduction to Excel Functions
What Are Functions?

Functions in Excel are predefined formulas that carry out particular computations or operations. They save you time and effort by automating complex calculations. To use a function:

1. Choose the cell in which you want the outcome.

2. Start by typing "=," followed by the function name (e.g., SUM).

3. Enter the required arguments (values or cell references).

4. Close the parentheses and press "Enter."

Performing Simple Calculations

Basic Arithmetic Operators

Excel supports basic arithmetic operations like addition (+), subtraction (-), multiplication (*), and division (/). To perform simple calculations:

1. Select a cell.

2. Type the formula using operators (e.g., "=A1+B1").

Order of Operations (BODMAS)

· Excel follows the BODMAS (Brackets, Orders, Division, Multiplication, Addition, Subtraction) rule when evaluating formulas with multiple operations. Use parentheses to specify the order.

AutoSum and Common Functions

AutoSum Function

AutoSum is a handy function for quickly adding up a range of numbers. To use AutoSum:

1. Select the cell where you want the total.

2. Click the "Σ" symbol (AutoSum) on the Home tab.

3. Excel will automatically select adjacent cells with data, or you can manually select the range.

SUM Function

A range of values is added up using the SUM function. To use SUM:

1. Select the cell where you want the total.

2. Enter "=SUM ("and the range of cells you want to add

3. Close the parentheses and press "Enter."

AVERAGE and MAX Functions

The AVERAGE function determines a range of numbers' average, and the MAX function finds the maximum value. To use these functions:

1. Select the cell for the result.

2. type "=AVERAGE ("or "=MAX("and select the range of cells you want to add.

3. Close the parentheses and press "Enter."

Absolute vs. Relative Cell References
Relative Cell References

Cell references in formulas are often relative by default. The references are changed appropriately when you duplicate a formula to another cell. As an illustration, if you duplicate a formula from cell C1 to C2, it will change from "=A1+B1" to "=A2+B2."

Absolute Cell References

Absolute cell references stay fixed when copied. You denote them with a "$" symbol. No matter where you replicate the formula, "A1" will always correspond to cell A1.

Mixed Cell References

Mixed references fix either the row or column while allowing the other to adjust. For example, "=$A1" locks the column reference but allows the row to change when copied horizontally.

In conclusion, by mastering the concepts and techniques covered in Chapter 2, you'll gain proficiency in creating and using functions and formulas in Excel. As you proceed through intermediate-level data analysis and automation jobs, this expertise will be helpful.

Chapter 3
Data Management

In this chapter, we'll focus on effectively managing and organizing data in Excel. These skills are essential for maintaining clean and structured datasets, which are crucial for analysis and reporting.

Sorting and Filtering Data

Sorting Data

Sorting arranges data in a specified order, making it easier to find and analyze information. To sort data:

1. Choose the range that you want to sort.

2. Select "Sort A to Z" or "Sort Z to A" from the Data tab buttons.

3. Customize sorting options as needed.

Filtering Data

Filtering allows you to display only specific rows of data based on criteria you define. To filter data:

1. Select the range containing your data.

2. On the Data tab, click the "Filter" option.

3. Use filter drop-down arrows to select criteria and narrow down your data.

Data Validation and Drop-down Lists

Data Validation

Data entry into cells is validated to ensure it complies with predetermined standards. To apply data validation:

1. Make a selection of the cell(s) you want to validate.

2. Click the Data tab and Select "Data Validation."

3. Define validation rules, such as number ranges or date formats.

4. Customize input messages and error alerts.

Creating Drop-down Lists

Drop-down lists allow users to select values from predefined options, reducing errors and ensuring data consistency. To create a drop-down list:

1. Choose the cell where the list should appear.

2. Navigate to the Data tab and choose "Data Validation."

3. Under the "Settings" tab, select "List" as the validation criteria.

4. Enter the list values or refer to a range with valid options.

Removing Duplicates

Identifying Duplicates

Duplicates can clutter your dataset and lead to inaccuracies. To identify duplicates:

1. Select the range containing your data.

2. Move to the Data tab and Select "Remove Duplicates."

3. Choose the columns to check for duplicates and click "OK."

Text-to-Columns

Splitting Text Using Text-to-Columns

Sometimes, data in a single cell must be split into multiple cells. To do this using Text-to-Columns:

1. Choose the cell or cells to split the text in.

2. Go to the Data tab and choose "Text-to-Columns."

3. Select the delimiter (e.g., space, comma) that separates the text.

4. Choose the destination where the split data should appear.

With the conclusion of this chapter, you've mastered the data management techniques covered. You'll become proficient in sorting and filtering data, ensuring data integrity through validation and drop-down lists, removing duplicates to maintain clean datasets, and using Text-to-Columns to manipulate text-based data effectively.

Chapter 4
Formatting For Clarity

We will explore various formatting techniques in Excel that enhance the visual clarity of your spreadsheets. Effective formatting not only makes data more presentable but also helps convey insights more effectively.

By mastering the formatting techniques covered in this chapter, you can transform your data into visually appealing and informative spreadsheets. Effective cell formatting, conditional formatting, custom cell styles, data bars, color scales, and icons will help you convey information more clearly and make your spreadsheets more accessible to everyone who looks at them.

Cell Formatting Essentials

Font Styles and Sizes

Excel provides a range of font styles and sizes to customize the appearance of your text. To change font styles and sizes:

1. Choose the cell or range that needs formatting.

2. Use the "Font" group on the Home tab to modify font settings.

Borders and Gridlines

Borders and gridlines help separate cells and sections, making your data more accessible to read. To add borders and gridlines:

1. Select the cells or range where you want to apply borders.

2. Use the "Borders" drop-down in the Font group to select border styles

Cell Fill Colors

Changing cell background colors can highlight specific data or categories. To change cell fill colors:

a. Choose the cells you want to format.

b. Use the "Fill Color" button in the Font group to choose a background color.

Conditional Formatting

Applying Conditional Formatting Rules

You can automatically format cells using conditional formatting if certain conditions are met. To apply conditional formatting:

1. Choose the range that you wish to format conditionally.

2. Go to the Home tab and choose "Conditional Formatting."

3. Select a rule type (e.g., Highlight Cells Rules, Top/Bottom Rules, Data Bars).

4. Define the formatting rule and criteria.

Creating Custom Conditional Formatting Rules

Custom conditional formatting rules enable you to set your conditions and formatting styles. To create custom rules:

1. Select the range.

2. Click the Home tab, select "Conditional Formatting," and select "New Rule."

3. Specify the rule formula and formatting.

Customizing Cell Styles

Cell Styles Overview

Cell styles are predefined combinations of font, fill color, and border settings that can be applied to cells for consistent formatting. To apply cell styles:

1. Choose the cell or range that needs formatting.

2. Go to the Home tab and choose a cell style from the Cell Styles group.

Creating Custom Cell Styles

Custom cell styles allow you to define your formatting styles for consistent use. To create custom cell styles:

1. Select a cell with the desired formatting.

2. Open the Cell Styles dialog box and click "New Cell Style."

3. Specify the formatting options for the new style.

Data Bars, Color Scales, and Icon Sets

Data Bars

Data bars are conditional formatting options that add horizontal bars within cells to represent data values. To use data bars:

1. Select the range.

2. Go to the Home tab, choose "Conditional Formatting,"

and select "Data Bars."

Color Scales

Color scales apply colors based on the relative values in a range, creating a gradient effect. To use color scales:

1. Select the range.

2. Go to the Home tab, choose "Conditional Formatting," and select "Color Scales."

Icon Sets

Icon sets add small icons to cells based on their values, aiding in quick data interpretation. To use icon sets:

1. Select the range.

2. Go to the Home tab, choose "Conditional Formatting," and select "Icon Sets."

Chapter 5
Charts And Graphs

In this chapter, we'll explore the world of charts and graphs. In Excel, Charts are powerful tools for visualizing data and conveying insights effectively.

By the end, you'll have a solid understanding of creating basic charts, customizing them to suit your needs, adding trendlines to reveal data trends, and using sparklines for quick, concise data visualization. These skills will empower you to present data effectively and make data-driven decisions with confidence.

Creating Basic Charts

Selecting Data for Charts

Before creating a chart, it's essential to select the data you want to represent graphically. To choose data for a chart:

1. Select the cells that have the information you want to add highlighted.

2. Include labels in the first row and columns to provide context.

Inserting a Chart

Excel offers various chart types, such as bar charts, line charts, pie charts, and more. To create a basic chart:

1. Select the data range.
2. Select the preferred chart type by going to the Insert tab.
3. Excel will generate a default chart on your worksheet.

Customizing Charts

Chart Elements

Charts can be customized extensively to convey the desired message. To customize chart elements:

1. To choose the chart, click on it.

2. Use the Chart Elements (+) button to add or remove chart elements like titles, data labels, and legends.

3. Right-click on any element to format it.

Formatting Chart Elements

Excel provides a range of formatting options to make your chart visually appealing. To format chart elements:

1. Select the chart element you want to format.
2. Right-click and choose "Format" to access formatting options.

Adding Trendlines

What are Trendlines?

Trendlines are used to identify and visualize trends in data. They are often used in line and scatter plots. To add a trendline:

1. Right-click on a data series in your chart.

2. Select "Add Trendline."

3. Choose the desired type (e.g., linear, exponential).

4. Customize options like display equation and R-squared value.

Sparklines for Quick Data Trends

Introduction to Sparklines

Sparklines are small mini-charts that fit within a single cell. They provide a quick visual summary of data trends. To create sparklines:

1. Select the cell where you want the sparkline.

2. Select the sparkline type (line, column, win/loss) under the Insert tab.

3. Select the data range you want to represent with the sparkline.

Chapter 6
Efficiency Boosters

In this chapter, we'll explore various shortcuts and formulas that can significantly enhance your efficiency while working.

Keyboard Shortcuts for Everyday Tasks

Why Keyboard Shortcuts?

Keyboard shortcuts are keystroke combinations that allow you to perform common tasks quickly without navigating menus or using the mouse. They can save you a significant amount of time and improve your workflow in Excel.

Essential Keyboard Shortcuts

Discover a selection of essential keyboard shortcuts for everyday tasks in Excel, such as:

· Copying, cutting, and pasting data.

· Undoing and redoing actions.

· Navigating worksheets and workbooks.

· Formatting cells and text.

List of Excel Shortcuts:

1. Ctrl + N: New Workbook

2. Ctrl + O: Open Workbook

3. Ctrl + S: Save Workbook

4. Ctrl + C: Copy

5. Ctrl + X: Cut

6. F11: Creates new chart on a new workbook

7. Ctrl + F2: Opens the print preview window

8. Ctrl + Shift + F12: Prints the current Worksheet

9. Ctrl + Shift + F11: Creates a chart of the selected data on a new worksheet

10. Ctrl + B: Applies or removes bold formatting.

11. Ctrl + V: Paste

12. Ctrl + Z: Undo

13. Ctrl + Y: Redo

14. Ctrl + F: Find

15. Ctrl + H: Replace

16. Ctrl + I: Italicizes the selected text

17. Ctrl + U: underlines the selected text

18. Ctrl + G: Opens the Go To dialog box

19. Ctrl + F6: Switches between open workbooks

20. Ctrl + F1: Hides or shows the ribbon

21. Ctrl + A: Select All

22. Ctrl + Space: Select Entire Column

23. Shift + Space: Select Entire Row

24. Ctrl + Shift + "+": Insert New Worksheet

25. Ctrl + F1: Show/Hide Ribbon

26. Alt + Enter: Start a New Line in a Cell

27. Alt + H + L: Opens conditioning formatting menu

28. Alt + H + L + N: Opens new rule dialog box

29. Alt + H + L + R: Opens the manage rule dialog box

30. Ctrl + Page Up/Down: Switch between Worksheets

31. Ctrl + Shift + F8: Selects or deselects cell for a macro

32. Ctrl + Shift + F3: Creates a new macro

33. Ctrl + Arrow Keys: Navigate to Edge of Data Region

34. F2: Edit Active Cell

35. Ctrl + Home: Go to Cell A1

36. Ctrl + End: Go to the Last Cell with the Data

37. Alt + E, S, V: Paste Special

38. F4: Repeat Last Action

39. Alt + Enter: Add Line Break within a Cell

40. Ctrl + 1: Format Cells Dialog Box

41. Ctrl +: Enter Current Date

42. Ctrl + Shift +: Enter Current Time

43. Alt + D, F, F: Insert Date Function

44. Alt + D, T, T: Insert Time Function

45. Alt + E, I, S: Flash Fill

46. Ctrl +: Navigate to Precedent Cells

47. Ctrl +: Navigate to Dependent Cells

48. Alt + D, P: Page Setup Dialog

49. Ctrl + P: Print

50. Alt + H, V, V: Paste Values

51. Ctrl + K: Insert Hyperlink

52. Ctrl + Tab: Switch Between Open Workbooks

53. Ctrl + W: Close Workbook

54. Ctrl + F4: Close Active Window

55. Alt + E, A, A: Clear All

56. Alt + Enter: Start New Line in a Cell

57. Alt + Down Arrow: Open Data Validation List

58. Ctrl + 5: Apply Strikethrough

59. Ctrl + 9: Hide Rows

60. Ctrl + 0: Hide Columns

61. Ctrl + Shift + "+": Insert New Row/Column

62. Ctrl + -: Delete Row/Column

63. Alt + Enter: Start New Line in a Cell

64. Alt + R, A, A: Remove Hyperlink

65. Alt + R, H, O: Clear Hyperlinks

66. Ctrl + D: Copies content of the cell above the current cell

67. Ctrl + R: Copies content of the cell to the left of the current cell.

68. Ctrl + Shift + N: Creates a new worksheet

69. Ctrl + Shift + F: Opens the find and replace dialog box

70. Ctrl + Shift + H: Opens the replace dialog box

71. Ctrl + Shift + $: Applies the currency format

72. Ctrl + Shift + %: Applies the percentage format

73. Ctrl + Shift + ~: Applies the general format

74. Ctrl + Shift + !: Applies a two-place decimal format to numbers

75. Ctrl + Shift + #: Applies date format with day, month, and year

76. Alt + =: Inserts the sum function

77. Ctrl + Shift + A: Inserts the average function

78. Ctrl + Shift + M: Inserts the MIN function

79. Ctrl + Shift + X: Inserts the MAX function

80. Ctrl + Shift + Arrow keys: Select the cell to the last cell in a row or column that contains data

81. Ctrl + Shift + End: Pick every cell in the worksheet with data, starting from the current cell and ending with the final cell.

82. Ctrl + Shift + L: Toggles filter on and off

83. Alt + W + Q: Zooms to 100%

84. Alt + W + X: Zooms to fit the selection

85. Ctrl + Mouse Scroll Wheel: Zooms in and out of the worksheet

86. Alt + W + S: splits the worksheet into panes

87. Alt + W + F: Freezes the top row of the worksheet

88. Alt + W + R: Freezes the first column of the worksheet

89. Alt + T + P + W: Opens the protect workbook dialog box

90. Alt + T + U + W: Opens the unprotect workbook dialog box

91. Alt + T + P: Opens the Protect sheet dialog box

92. Alt + T + U: Opens the Unprotect Sheet dialog box

93. Alt + D + L: Opens the data validation dialog box

94. Alt + D + L + V: Opens the data validation dialog box with the criteria tab selected

95. Alt + D + L + S: Opens the data validation dialog box with the settings tab selected

96. Ctrl +]: Selects all cells that refer to the active cell

97. Ctrl + [: Selects all cells that are referred to by the active cell

98. Ctrl + Shift + o}: chooses every cell that mentions the active cell, whether directly or indirectly

99. Ctrl + Shift {: selects all cells that are directly or indirectly referred to by the active cell

100. Alt + J + T + F: Opens the PivotTable Field List

Excel Formulas:

Basic Functions:

1. =SUM (select the range of cells): Adds numbers in a range.

2. =AVERAGE (select the range of cells): Calculates the average of numbers in a range.

3. =MAX (select the range of cell): Returns the maximum value in a range.

4. =MIN (select the range of cell): Returns the minimum value in a range.

5. =COUNT (select the range of cell): Counts the number of cells with data.

6. =IF(F1>10, "Yes", "No"): Conditional function.

Math and Statistical Functions:

7. =RAND (): Generates a random number between 0 and 1.

8. =RANDBETWEEN (1, 100): Generates a random number between specified values

9. =ROUND (K1, 2): Rounds a number to a specified number of decimal places.

10. =SUMIF (L1:L10, ">50"): Sums values based on a condition.

11. =AVERAGEIF (M1:M10, "<30"): Averages values based on a condition.

12. =COUNTIF (N1:N10, "Apple"): Counts cells based on a condition.

Logical Functions:

13. IF(A2>B2, "True", "False"): Basic IF statement.

14. =AND (C2>10, D2<20): Checks if multiple conditions are true.

15. =OR (E2="Red", E2="Blue"): Checks if any condition is true.

16. =NOT (F2="Yes"): Reverses the result of a logical test.

Basic Excel Tips

Some Excel quick tips and tricks to help you work more efficiently and effectively

1. **Autofill:** Double-click the fill handle (bottom right corner of a cell) to copy down a formula or series quickly.

2. **Cell Navigation:** Use Ctrl + Arrow keys to jump to the edge of data regions in your worksheet.

3. **Quickly Select Data:** Ctrl + Shift + Arrow keys selects data in all directions.

4. **Multi-Select Sheets:** Ctrl + Click on sheet tabs to select multiple sheets.

5. **Resize Columns and Rows:** Double-click the border between column or row headers to auto-fit the content.

6. **Split Text:** Use Text to Columns (Data > Text to Columns) to split text in a cell into multiple cells.

7. **Remove Duplicates:** Remove duplicate values from a range using Data > Remove Duplicates.

8. **Flash Fill:** Excel can recognize patterns in your data; use Ctrl + E (Windows) or Cmd + E (Mac) to apply Flash Fill.

9. **Insert Current Date/Time:** Ctrl + ; inserts the current date; Ctrl + Shift + ; inserts the current time.

10. **Quickly Add Rows/Columns:** Right-click a row or column header and choose "Insert" to add a new row/column.

11. **Remove Error Cells in Large Data**: Follow these steps: Navigate to Home Tab ➜ Editing ➜ Find & Replace Go To Special. In the Go To dialog box, choose 'formula' and check 'errors.' Click OK to select all errors, then delete them with the 'Delete' button

Formatting Tips:

11. **Cell Styles:** Use Cell Styles (Home > Cell Styles) for consistent formatting.

12. **Custom Number Formats:** Create custom number formats (Format Cells > Number > Custom) for specialized display.

13. **Freeze Panes:** Use View > Freeze Panes to lock rows or columns while scrolling.

14. **Conditional Formatting:** Apply conditional formatting (Home > Conditional Formatting) to highlight data based on rules.

15. **Remove Formatting:** Use Ctrl + Space to select a column and then Ctrl + Space again to select the entire sheet, then Ctrl + Space a third time to choose the entire sheet, and finally, Ctrl + Space one last time to select only data columns.

16. **Data Bars:** Use data bars in conditional formatting for visualizing data in a cell.

17. **Formula Auditing:** Use formulas like =FORMULATEXT () and =CELL () to debug complex formulas.

Data Entry and Management:

18. **Data Validation:** Apply data validation (Data > Data Validation) to restrict user input to specific values.

19. **Transpose Data:** Use Paste Special (Ctrl + Alt + V) to transpose rows and columns.

20. **Filter Data:** Use the Filter button to filter data in a range quickly.

21. **Data Tables:** Create Data Tables (Insert > Table) to make data management and analysis easier.

22. **Quick Analysis:** Select data and use the Quick Analysis button in the bottom right corner to access various tools.

23. Excel **Tables:** Use Excel Tables (Insert > Table) for dynamic ranges and easier data manipulation.

24. Text **to Columns:** Split data in a column into multiple columns using Text to Columns (Data > Text to Columns).

Keyboard Shortcuts:

25. **Quick Save:** Ctrl + S to save your workbook.

26. **Quick Copy:** Ctrl + C to copy selected cells; Ctrl + X to cut; Ctrl + V to paste.

27. **Undo and Redo:** Ctrl + Z to undo; Ctrl + Y to redo.

28. **Find and Replace:** Ctrl + F to open Find; Ctrl + H to open Find and Replace.

29. **Formula Bar:** F2 to edit a cell's content in the Formula Bar.

Charting and Graphs:

30. **Create Charts:** Select data and use the "Insert Chart" button to create charts.

31. **Combo Charts:** Combine different chart types in a single chart.

32. **Chart Templates:** Save chart templates for consistent formatting.

33. **Sparklines:** Use Sparklines to create small, in-cell charts.

34. **Secondary Axes:** Add a secondary axis to your charts for better data visualization.

These shortcuts, formulas, tips, and tricks should help you become more proficient in Excel and streamline your work processes. Remember to adjust these examples to your specific needs and data. Also, remember that practice and experimentation are key to becoming an Excel expert.